THE "LOOK ABOUT YOU" Nature Study Books

BOOK III

THE "LOOK ABOUT YOU" Nature Study Books

BOOK III

by

Thomas W. Hoare

YESTERDAY'S CLASSICS

ITHACA, NEW YORK

Cover and arrangement © 2019 Yesterday's Classics, LLC.

This edition, first published in 2019 by Yesterday's Classics, an imprint of Yesterday's Classics, LLC, is an unabridged republication of the text originally published by T. C. & E. C. Jack. For the complete listing of the books that are published by Yesterday's Classics, please visit www.yesterdaysclassics.com. Yesterday's Classics is the publishing arm of Gateway to the Classics which presents the complete text of hundreds of classic books for children at www.gatewaytotheclassics.com.

ISBN: 978-1-63334-111-1

Yesterday's Classics, LLC
PO Box 339
Ithaca, NY 14851

CONTENTS

- I. Birds in Winter....................1
- II. Seed-Eaters and Insect-Eaters...6
- III. Buds.........................10
- IV. A Baby Plant..................16
- V. How a Plant Grows..............21
- VI. More about Seeds..............29
- VII. The Horse Pond in Spring.....33
- VIII. Uncle George's Tank.........39
- IX. Tadpoles......................44
- X. Frogs, Toads, and Newts........49
- XI. Underground Stems.............55
- XII. Caterpillars.................62
- XIII. The White Butterfly.........70
- XIV. The Toiling Caddis...........76
- Appendix.........................83
  - Hints to Teachers..............83
  - Exercises......................88

PREFACE

Every lesson herein set down has, during the author's many years' experience in teaching Nature Study, been taught by observation and practice again and again; and each time with satisfactory result. The materials required for most of the lessons—whether they be obtained from the naturalist-dealer or from the nearest hedge, ditch, or pond—are within everybody's reach.

There is nothing that appeals to the heart of the ordinary child like *living things*, be they animal or vegetable, and there is no branch of education at the present day that bears, in the young mind, such excellent fruit as the study of the simple, living things around us.

Your child is nothing if not curious. He wants to understand everything that lives and moves and has its being in his bright little world.

Nature Study involves so many ingenious little deductions, that the reasoning powers are almost constantly employed, and intelligence grows proportionately. The child's powers of observation are stimulated, and his memory is cultivated in the way most pleasing to his inquiring nature. By dissecting seeds, bulbs, buds, and flowers, his hand is trained, and methods expeditious and exact are inculcated. By drawing his specimens, no matter how roughly or rapidly, his eye is trained more thoroughly than any amount of enforced copying of stiff, uninteresting models of prisms, cones, etc., ever could train it.

The love of flowers and animals is one of the most commendable traits in the disposition of the wondering child, and ought to be encouraged above all others.

It is the author's fondest and most sanguine hope that the working out of the exercises, of which this booklet is mainly composed, may prove much more of a joy than a task, and that the practical knowledge gained thereby may tempt his little readers to study further the great book of Nature, whose broad pages are ever open to us, and whose silent answers to our manifold questions are never very difficult to read.

T. W. H.

Birds in Winter

CHAPTER I

BIRDS IN WINTER

"When we look out there, it makes us feel thankful that we have a nice cosy room to play in and a warm fire to sit beside."

It was Uncle George who spoke. His two nephews, Frank and Tom, stood at the window watching the birds feeding outside, while Dolly, their little sister, was busy with her picture-blocks on the carpet.

"Yes, it is better to be inside in winter," said Frank, the elder boy. "These poor little birds must have a hard time out in the cold all night."

"I should not mind being a bird during the rest of the year, though," said little Tom. "It must be so jolly to be able to fly wherever you like."

Uncle George smiled, and said, "Birds are very happy little creatures, Tom, but they have many enemies. Their lives are in constant danger. They must always be on the look-out for cats, hawks, guns, and cruel boys. Those birds that stay with us all the year round have often a hard fight for life in winter-time. In fact, many of them starve to death.

"Most of our birds fly to warmer countries in autumn, and come back to us in spring. These miss the frost and snow, but a great number of them get drowned while crossing the sea. I think, as a little boy, you are much better off.

"Let me see; have you put out any food for the birds this morning?"

"Yes, Uncle George, we have done exactly as you told us," said Frank. "Mother made a little net, which we filled with suet and scraps of meat for the tomtits. We hung it on the ivy, quite near the window. We also put plenty of crumbs and waste bits from the kitchen on the space you cleared for the birds yesterday."

"Very good," said Uncle George, "and I see your feathered friends are busy in both places."

He looked out and saw a crowd of birds hopping on the frozen lawn round the well-filled dish. The little net, which hung just outside the window, was alive with hungry tomtits. They pecked eagerly at the suet, and chattered their thanks between every mouthful.

"What a lot of birds we have to-day," Uncle George remarked. "Do you know the names of them all, boys?"

"We know those you pointed out to us yesterday," said Frank. "There is the chaffinch, the thrush, the greenfinch, the blackbird, and the hedge-sparrow, but I don't know that one with the bright red breast, black velvet head, and grey wings. And there is a new one among the tomtits. He has a very long tail, and is like a small parrot."

"Oh," said Uncle George, "the first you spoke of is the bullfinch. He is so easily tamed that he makes a splendid pet. The hen bullfinch is there too, I see. She has a dull brown breast, and is not quite so pretty as her husband. The bullfinch is very fond of berries. If we could get some hawthorn or rowan berries, we should have all the bullfinches in the district around us. The other bird is the long-tailed tit. He is also a very amusing little chap."

Bullfinches

"Why do the tomtits make such a fuss about the suet?" asked Tom. "The bullfinches do not come near it."

"That is because the tomtit is a flesh-eater, Tom. He lives on insects. The bullfinch feeds on berries and seeds. He is also blamed for eating the young buds of fruit-trees in spring-time, but I am not quite sure that he does this."

"Where are all the insects in winter, Uncle George?" asked Frank.

"Well, most of them are buried deep in the ground. Some of them are tucked up in warm cases, and hidden in the chinks of trees and walls."

"Then why don't the birds that feed on insects search those trees and walls for them?" Frank asked.

"So the birds do, but the sleeping insects are very hard to find. The cases which hold them are often coloured exactly like the tree or wall which they are fixed to; so that even the sharp eyes of a hungry bird cannot see them."

CHAPTER II

SEED-EATERS AND INSECT-EATERS

The snow did not go away for some days. While it lasted, Frank and Tom watched the birds very closely. They learned many new and curious things about them.

The sparrows and robins had grown so tame that they would fly right up to the window-sill, and eat the crumbs and seeds that were placed there for them; while the tomtits paid great attention to the little net bag that hung quite close to the window. So long as they stood back a short distance from the window, the two boys could watch the funny tricks of these hungry little visitors.

Tomtits

Amongst other things, they learned to tell a seed-eating bird from one that feeds on insects.

SEED-EATERS AND INSECT-EATERS

Seed-eating birds, as their uncle told them, have short, stout, hard bills, just the thing for shelling seeds. The insect-eaters have longer and more slender bills; while birds that live upon both seeds and insects have bills hard enough to shell seeds and yet long and sharp enough to pick insects out of their hiding-places.

So many birds came to the feast, that Uncle George cleared the snow from another part of the lawn and spread some dry ashes upon it. Upon one patch he scattered seeds and crumbs, and on the other he placed a large flat dish.

In this dish were put all sorts of waste scraps from the kitchen, such as bones, potatoes, and pieces of meat. Uncle George did this so that the boys could tell flesh-eating birds from those that lived upon seeds.

The starlings came to the dish first, and fought among themselves for the food, although there was much more than enough for them all.

Starling

Then came a few rooks, who walked about the dish in quite a lordly way. Every now and again one of them would seize a huge crust of bread or a potato in his clumsy bill and fly with it a short distance away. The starlings, thrushes, and blackbirds hopped nimbly about, picking up a choice morsel here and there.

The new patch was often crowded with finches of all kinds. The boys noticed that many of the birds fed at both places. Among these were sparrows, robins, chaffinches, thrushes, and starlings. These birds, their uncle explained to them, fed on a mixed food of insects, seeds, and fruits.

Rook

It amused them very much to watch how the rooks and jackdaws always dragged the food away from the dish, as if they were stealing it; while now and then a blackbird would fly away with a loud chatter, as if he had been suddenly found out whilst doing something very wrong.

"These birds," said Uncle George, "are looked upon as enemies by farmers and gardeners. They are scared out of our fields and gardens by every possible means. That is what makes them steal even the food that is given to them."

"But they pick the newly-sown seeds out of the ground, and steal the fruit when it is ripe," said Frank. "That is what the gardener says."

"If the gardener only knew how much they help him, by eating up the grubs and beetles that damage his plants, he would not grudge them a few seeds and berries, Frank," Uncle George replied. "The rook is one of the farmer's best friends; and if it were not for thrushes, starlings, blackbirds, and such insect-eating birds, our gardens would be overrun with insects. If these insects were allowed to increase, we should not be able to grow anything. Even the sparrow is the gardener's friend. He eats the caterpillars that would spoil our fruit trees and bushes."

CHAPTER III

BUDS

Uncle George and the two boys had been for a long walk. They brought home a lot of twigs which they had cut from trees at the roadside.

Uncle George placed some of these twigs in bottles filled with water. These bottles were placed in the window, so that they could get plenty of sunlight. The rest of the twigs were laid upon the table.

"Now, boys," said Uncle George, "we are going to find out what buds are. Here is a twig of the horse-chestnut tree, and here is one of the beech tree. Do you notice any difference between them?"

"Oh, yes," said Frank, "they are very different. The beech buds are longer."

"Anything else?" his uncle asked.

"The horse-chestnut buds have sticky stuff all over them," said Tom.

"Quite right," said Uncle George. "On the beech twig the buds are placed singly on opposite sides. On the horse-chestnut twig the buds are in pairs."

BUDS

Then Uncle George cut one of the buds through with his knife, and they saw that a great number of thick scales were folded round a little green thing in the centre. They saw also a mass of woolly stuff between the scales and the little green object.

Twigs of Beech and Chestnut, showing Buds

Uncle George gave each of the boys a twig, and showed them how to take the scales off the top bud with a large needle. The outside scales were not easily removed. They were so sticky—they stuck to everything that touched them, and soon the boys' fingers were covered with the sticky stuff. As they went on with their work, they found out that the inner scales were not sticky. At last they got all the scales off, and there was nothing left but a tiny woolly mass. On teasing out, this woolly bundle was found to be a little branch bearing small leaves. Every part of it was covered with wool.

"Now," said Uncle George, "you can perhaps tell me what a bud is."

"It is just a little baby branch, snugly tucked up in a tiny blanket and well covered over with many scale-leaves," said Frank.

"Very good," said Uncle George. "Now tell me why it is tucked up in this warm blanket, and perhaps Tom can tell us what the sticky stuff on the outer scales is for."

"I am sure I cannot tell," said Frank.

"Just think," said his uncle kindly. "Why did you call it a *baby* branch? Is it because it is so small, or because it is so snugly wrapped up? Why are babies wrapped up in soft warm clothing?"

"Oh, I know now," said Frank, "The woolly stuff is to keep out the winter cold."

"And the sticky stuff on the outside," said Tom, "must be for keeping out the rain."

"You are both right," said Uncle George. "Buds are formed in autumn and early winter. They are, as you have seen, very tender little things. Frost or wet would kill them. But rolled up in soft woolly clothing, covered in with many thick scale-leaves, and made quite waterproof by a thick coat of the sticky stuff, they do not fear the cold.

"If you look at your twigs again, you will find that in taking off the scales you have left a thick ring of marks right round the twig.

"Now, if you look down the twig, you will notice another ring of such marks. These are the scale-marks of last year's bud. The part of the twig in between these two ring marks is a year's growth."

"There is a third ring on mine farther down the stem," said Frank.

"Yes, and another farther down still," said Uncle George. "These are the bud marks of former years. Let us measure the distance between them, for in this way we can tell the kind of summers we have had in past years.

"Last year's growth, you see, is two inches. The growth of the year before is three inches, and the one beneath that is four and a half inches. This tells us that there was very little sunshine during last summer or the summer before, and that three years ago there was a warm summer, causing much growth."

"I see some other strange marks on the twig," said Tom.

"Oh, you mean the horse-shoe marks. These are the scars left by the big green leaves which fell off in autumn. You will find one of these curious horse-shoe marks under each bud.

"Here is a hawthorn twig. I brought it to let you see another way in which plants protect their buds. In the hawthorn the buds usually occur in pairs together. Between each pair of buds there is a long sharp thorn.

Plants protected by Thorns and Prickles

BUDS

"The reason why every pair of buds is guarded in this way is very clear. The horse-chestnut and beech have tall, stout stems, which rear up their branches far out of the reach of grazing animals. The hawthorn is a low growing tree. Its branches are within easy reach, and its tender buds would be nipped off by sheep and cattle if it were not for these sharp thorns.

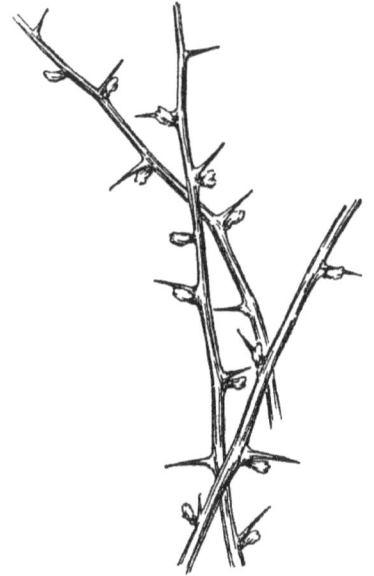

Hawthorn Twigs

"The thorns also prevent the buds from being knocked off by anything rubbing against the hawthorn hedge. You will notice that each thorn is very much longer than the buds beside it. These thorns can give a very cruel prick, as every boy knows who has tried to cut a twig from the hawthorn hedge.

"By and by we shall see that there are many plants which arm themselves against animals in this way."

CHAPTER IV

A BABY PLANT

"To-day," said Uncle George, "we are going to try to find out something about seeds." And he placed upon the table a saucerful of beans which had been soaking in water for two days.

"First let us look at the seeds as they are when we get them from the shop," he said, laying a handful of hard, wrinkled beans upon the table.

"They are as hard as stones, and very much smaller than those we soaked," said Frank.

"Yes, that is one thing we have learned about them already. Seeds take in water and swell greatly." As he spoke, Uncle George gave Frank, Tom, and Dolly each a small knife and a needle mounted in a handle. He then laid a small magnifying glass on the table.

"Take a soaked bean and look at it well," he said. "First we will look at the outside of it, then we will see what it has inside."

"My bean is covered all over with a smooth skin," said Dolly.

"And there is a long black mark on one side of it," Tom added.

"Come on, Frank," said his uncle, "haven't you got something to say?"

"It is sort of kidney-shaped," said Frank.

"Nothing more?"

Frank shook his head.

"Squeeze it," said Uncle George, "and tell me what you see."

"Oh, there is water oozing out of a little hole at the end of the black mark," said Frank.

"That shows us that the seed is not quite covered by its skin," said their uncle. "That little hole is there to allow a tiny root to grow out.

"Now let us remove the skin, or skins rather, for there are two of them. Begin as far away from the black mark as you can. You see that the outer skin is tough like leather, while the inner one is soft and silky. Now, if you pull the skins off gently, you will find something like a stout little root pointing towards the little hole you have already noticed. If you look at the edge of the seed you will notice a thin line or crack. Putting the knife into this crack, we find that the seed consists chiefly of two large, flat, white parts or lobes, with a very small object in between them. Let us remove one of these white masses, and have a look at this small object with the glass."

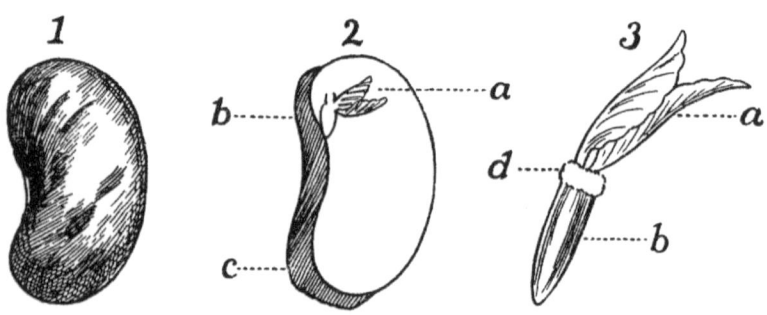

Seed of Runner Bean

*(1) outside; (2) inside; (3) baby plant, enlarged.
a, shoot; b, root; c, seed coat or skin;
d, junction of seed-leaves.*

Each of the children had a look through the glass in turn.

"Why," said Tom, "it is very like what we found inside the horse-chestnut bud. I can see two tiny leaves."

"Remove the little object on the point of your needle and look at it again," said Uncle George. "It has got something that your little horse-chestnut shoot did not have, I think."

"There is a little thing like a root," said Tom.

"It is a little plant with a very fat little root," said Frank.

"That is just what it is," said his uncle.

"Has every seed got a little plant inside it, Uncle George?" Dolly asked.

"Every seed, Dolly, no matter how small."

Uncle George split up one of the hard seeds that had

not been soaked, and showed them a little plant of the same kind inside; but it was so hard and brittle that he could crumble it up into powder between his fingers.

"And what are the two large white lobes for?" asked Frank.

"These are the seed-leaves. They are stores of plant-food. The young plant is fed by these until its root grows far down into the soil and its shoot grows high up into the air—until it is old enough and strong enough to find food for itself, in fact.

"In the bud, the little shoot is fed by the sap of the mother-plant. Here, in the seed, we have a baby plant wrapped up in two coats, one thick and leathery and the other soft and warm; and, in place of a large feeding-bottle, there are two huge masses of plant-food wrapped up with it."

"Why do we put seeds in the ground to make them grow?" asked Frank.

"A seed requires three things to make it grow. These three things are—*water*, *air*, and *warmth*. We can grow seeds without soil at all if we give them these three things. But if either water, air, or warmth be wanting, your seeds cannot grow."

"That is why seeds won't grow outside in winter, then," said Frank.

"That is the reason," his uncle answered. "In winter there is not enough heat to make seeds grow. If you sow seeds in a pot of dry soil in summer, and do not give them water, they will not grow."

"I think a seed is a most wonderful thing," said Tom.

"It is," said Uncle George, "wonderful indeed. The most wonderful thing about it is that there is life in it—sleeping life, awaiting these three things I have told you about.

"Dried up, and as hard as a stone, it will keep for years; but when air, warmth, and moisture are given it, it springs into life and becomes a plant, which grows, produces seeds, and dies.

"Now, we will plant the rest of the soaked beans—not in ground, for I want to let you see that the seed-leaves contain far more food than the tiny plant requires to feed it until it is old enough to take care of itself.

"We will plant these seeds in damp sawdust, from which they can get no food. We will see that they get water, air, and warmth, but no food except what is in the big seed-leaves."

Uncle George then got a box filled with sawdust, and placed the beans in it. He arranged them in different ways. Some beans he placed edgeways, others longways, others lying on their sides.

"I am doing this," he said, "to show you that, no matter how a seed happens to lie in the soil, its root will always grow down and its shoot will always grow up."

He then covered them up with a thin layer of sawdust, and placed the box in a warm corner of the kitchen. The boys promised to water the seeds every day, and to watch them as they grew.

CHAPTER V

HOW A PLANT GROWS

Every day the boys watched their buds and seeds bursting into life.

It was slow work; but, as winter passed slowly away and they were able to go out for walks more often, they had much to amuse them. They brought home all sorts of curious things, and soon had quite a host of living things to watch.

Three weeks passed before the horse-chestnut buds showed any signs of opening. By this time they had swelled out very much. First the sticky scales moved apart, then folded themselves backwards out of the way, and at last fell off altogether.

This moving apart of the scales was caused by the shoot or branch inside the bud, which was growing rapidly.

Before the scales fell off, it had burst its way through them. It was now a large mass of thick leaves all folded together, and covered all over with a sort of wool.

Soon these thick leaves moved apart, the woolly covering came off, and what a month ago was a little woolly body, so tiny that it had to be picked apart with a needle, was now a large stout branch, smooth and green, and bearing beautiful broad leaves.

Four Stages in the Opening of Horse-Chestnut Buds

Some of the buds brought forth small clusters of little green balls. These the boys at first thought were berries, but they afterwards found out that they were flowers.

After all the buds had quite opened out, they began slowly to wither. Uncle George told them the reason of this. It was because the branch had been cut away from the mother-tree, which drew its food from the soil and air.

The growing buds had used up all the sap which the cut branch contained.

Hedge and Trees in Early Spring

But by the time their twigs had withered, the buds outside had began to open—for spring was now at hand.

The hedges were becoming greener every day. The birds were heard singing in the woods, and little green shoots were springing up everywhere under foot.

Frank and Tom brought home opening buds of all kinds, and watched the hedges and trees as they walked daily to school.

Two of the bean seeds were dug up out of the sawdust every second or third day. In this way the boys were able to see exactly how a bean plant grows from seed.

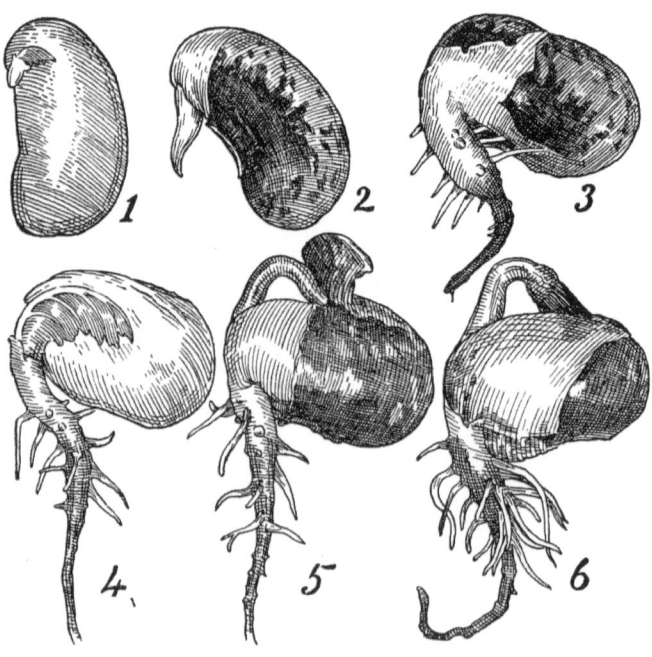

Stages in the Germination of the Runner Bean
In 1 and 4, inside of seed,
growing baby plant is shown.

HOW A PLANT GROWS

First the seed swells out; then the skin bursts, and the little plant in between the two masses of plant-food begins to grow.

The root always grows down straight. The little shoot always grows upwards.

After the root has grown about an inch it begins to branch; and in about two weeks these branch-roots are searching the soil for food all around the main root.

The shoot meanwhile is growing in length and thickness. It remains folded up until it reaches the air and light. Then its leaves open out and turn from a creamy colour to bright green.

One small box of seeds was placed in a dark cupboard. These beans grew much more quickly than those grown in the light; but they were pale, lank, and sickly. They never turned green.

From this the boys learned that the green colour of leaves and stems is due to the action of light.

Uncle George took a few grains of wheat and placed them upon wet blotting-paper. A tumbler turned upside down was placed over them.

In a few days the children saw that a few small roots had grown out from the end of each grain.

When these roots had grown to about half an inch in length, great tufts of long slender hairs sprang out all round them near their tips. These, their uncle told them, were "root-hairs."

The root-hairs of a plant are so fine that they are

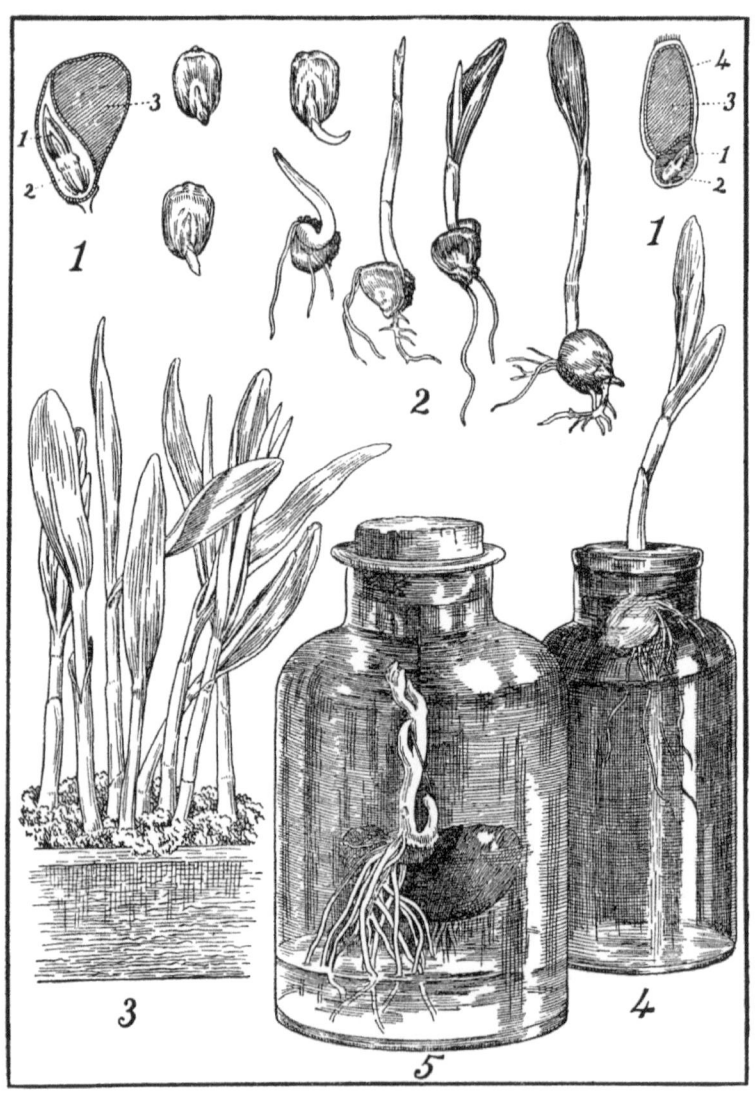

1. Magnified sections of Maize and Wheat Seeds, showing Young Plant, Food Store, etc.
2. Germination of Maize
3. Maize growing in Sawdust
4. Maize growing in Tap Water
5. Bean growing in Bottle over Water

always torn off when we dig or pull a plant out of the ground. It is by means of these slender root-hairs that the plant is able to suck water out of the soil; and this water always contains a very little plant-food in it.

The boys noticed that the wheat grain did not sprout in the same way as the bean seed. Instead of one stout little root, three usually came out. The tiny shoot seemed to grow from the *outside* of the grain, and the two large masses of plant-food were missing.

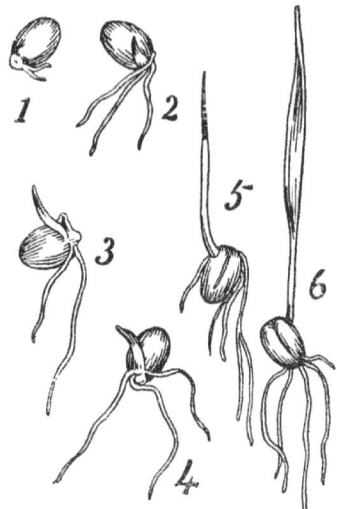

Stages in the Germination of Wheat

Some wheat seeds were soaked and cut down the middle. With the aid of the glass, the boys saw that in the wheat seed the baby plant is attached to *one* large mass of plant-food, made up of flour with an outside layer of bran.

Their uncle then told them that all the flowering plants in the world are of two great families, namely, those whose seeds have only one food store, like the wheat grain, and those whose seeds have two, like the bean.

*Plants that grow like maize.
These plants have but one food mass
in each of their seeds.*

CHAPTER VI

MORE ABOUT SEEDS

It was raining in torrents outside, and the boys were a little upset inside, for it was Saturday. They always looked forward to Saturday, for it was their great rambling day.

"I'm afraid we can't get out to-day," said Frank, sadly.

"I'm afraid not," said his uncle. "But that is no reason why we should sulk. We have those maize seeds to look over, you know, and by the time we have done that perhaps the rain will have stopped."

While Frank and Tom were bringing the boxes of seeds, Uncle George and Dolly were busy getting out knives, glasses, mounted needles, and the books they made their notes and sketches in.

There were four small boxes in all. Each box had been sown with maize or Indian corn at times a week apart, so that the plants in one box were five weeks old, in the next four weeks old, and so on.

"We will begin as we did with the bean. Let us cut the seed open first." As he spoke, Uncle George laid some soaked maize seeds on the table.

"If you look at these seeds carefully, you will notice a large mark on one of the flat sides of each."

"I see it," said Frank. "It is shaped something like a cone, and its broad end is at the narrow end of the seed."

"It is lighter in colour than the rest of the seed," said Tom.

"You are both right," said their uncle. "Now I want you to cut the seed longways, right down through the middle of that mark. Then use your glass, and tell me what you see.

"Look closely," said Uncle George, "first into one half and then into the other."

"Oh, I see something like a tiny plant," said Tom. "It is shut off from a great mass of what looks like plant-food, just like our wheat grains."

Tom made a rough sketch of it, and showed it to his uncle.

"That is the baby plant, and the great mass above it is plant-food," said his uncle.

"Come on, Frank. Don't let Tom do all the finding out. What have you to say?"

"The maize seed has only one mass of plant-food, and it does not seem to have two seed coats like the bean," Tom replied.

"You are right," said Uncle George; "but if you look again you will see that there is a thick layer of food stuff outside, which is of a different colour from the rest.

MORE ABOUT SEEDS

"This is like the bran layer which is round the food store in the wheat grain.

"This food store is starch, or, as we call it, *flour*.

"Now, let us look at the growing seeds. We will take a few seeds out of each box and see how they differ.

"The seeds in this box, the last sown, are just a week old. You see the root and shoot are just beginning to show.

"Make a sketch, drawing it as large as you can, and write under it, 'Maize seed after a week's growth.'

"Do the same with a seed from each of the other three boxes, and when you have drawn them all, tell me of any differences you notice between the growth of maize and that of the bean."

"They do not grow in the same way at all," said Frank, as he drew his last sketch. "In the maize seed the baby plant seems to be stuck on to one of the flat sides of the seed."

"What about the roots, Frank?"

"Oh yes, I see that," Frank went on. "The root branches out all at once in the maize seed. In some of these seeds the main root has scarcely grown at all. Their roots are all branch-roots."

"And, in the oldest plants, one great leaf rolls round the shoot and hides it," said Tom. "In the bean shoot we saw two leaves quite plainly."

"Quite right, Tom. Now, boys, compare your drawings with those you made of the bean. I will grow a maize and a bean seed together, so that you can watch the growth of both, and compare them day by day."

Uncle George then got an empty pickle bottle, and poured some water into it. Then he took a soaked bean seed, and, having run a thread through it with a needle, he hung it inside the bottle. He then corked the bottle, and placed it in the window.

He next took an old lamp chimney, and made a roll of blotting-paper to fit the inside of it. This roll of paper was stuffed with moss. A few maize seeds were pushed in between the glass and the paper, and the lamp chimney was placed in a saucerful of water in the window.

"Now, boys," said Uncle George, "I want you to watch these seeds every day. If you do so, you will learn how a seed grows into a plant; and you will learn this not from me, but from the plant itself."

Uncle George filled a wide bottle with water from the tap, and fixed one of the five-week-old maize plants in it by means of a split cork.

"I want you to watch this plant growing," he said, as he placed the bottle in the window. "You ought to draw it once a week. Most people think that plants draw their food chiefly from the soil. This is a great mistake.

"Plants take most of their food from the air, as you will see if you watch the growth of this plant. Of course, it has a good food store in the seed; but I think you will be surprised at the growth it makes from that food store, the bottle of tap water, and the air."

CHAPTER VII

THE HORSE POND IN SPRING

When Frank and Tom came home from school one afternoon, they found their uncle very busy finishing a net he had made of green gauze.

It had the shape of a shallow bag, and was fixed to a stout wire ring. This ring was fastened to a walking-stick with a piece of strong string.

On the table there were three wide glass jars, each with a piece of cord tied round the neck to serve as a handle.

"Now," said Uncle George, as he finished tying the net to the stick, "now we are all ready for a visit to that pond of yours."

Pond-Net and Glass Jars

The pond was about half a mile away, in the corner of a field near a wood. A small stream ran out of it, and joined a larger one a short distance away. The last time the boys had seen this pond it was covered with ice, and they had a merry time skating upon it. When they reached it on this afternoon, it looked quite different. The grass around its banks was fresh and green, and rushes were peeping up through the water.

"Listen!" said Uncle George.

"*Croak, croak, cr-roak*" came from beyond the rushes, while here and there a little head would bob up and down in the water.

"Frogs!" said Frank.

Uncle George nodded, and, stepping to the edge of the pond, he pulled the net out, and with it a large mass of what looked like clear jelly, having a large number of black dots in it.

"Bring the largest jar, Tom," he said, "we are going to take this home."

"What is it, Uncle George?" both boys asked at once.

"It is a mass of frog's eggs, called the spawn of the frog," their uncle replied. "Now, Frank, hold the jar over the water while I try to pour it in."

It was no easy matter getting it into the jar. It fell back into the pond several times before it was at last got in the jar.

"There," said Uncle George, as he placed the jar, now filled with frog spawn, upon the bank. "Now, let us go

THE HORSE POND IN SPRING

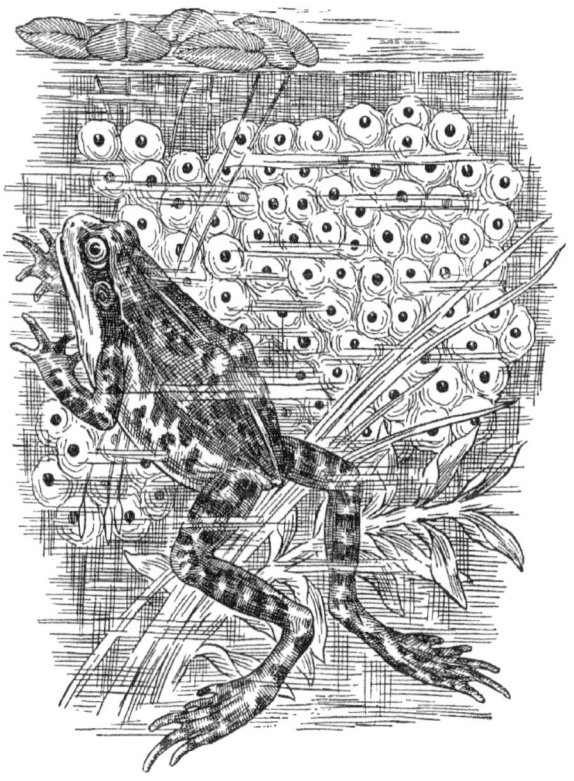

Frog and Spawn in Water

to another part of the pond and look for something else.

"Keep quite still and look into the water. That is the only way to study pond life. If you move about you will see very little. Now tell me if you see anything moving at the bottom of the pond."

"I see things like little pieces of stick moving slowly about," said Tom in a whisper; "but perhaps it is the water that is moving them."

"Not a bit of it," said Uncle George. "They are not pieces of stick. There is a living creature inside each of them. We must have some of them, Tom. They are very interesting creatures." And Uncle George put his hand carefully down and picked several of them up.

"These are caddis 'worms,'" said Uncle George. He placed them in the second jar, and filled it up with water.

Tom then saw that each of the "sticks" was really a little house, in which was an insect of some sort.

The cases were built of all kinds of odds and ends, glued together by the clever creatures that lived inside them.

Some were built of little pieces of rush or water-weed, others of tiny shells, and others of very small stones.

Each case was open at one end, and from this end the little dweller came almost half-way out. They could see his head, his legs, and the fore part of his body as he moved along, dragging his little house after him.

"Uncle George, come here please," Frank shouted from the other side of the pond. "Oh, such a funny animal—a fish with legs."

"A fish with legs?" said Uncle George, laughing. "Oh, we must come and see that."

"Why, that isn't a fish, Frank. It is a newt." And Uncle George put in the net to catch him. But the creature was too quick for him. It darted out of sight.

"Here are two others. Oh, such big ones," said Tom, in a loud whisper.

This time Uncle George was luckier. When he drew

The Horse Pond in Spring

up the net there were two large creatures like lizards in it.

"This is a lucky find, boys," said their uncle. "Great crested newts, and what beauties they are!"

The boys were surprised to see him take one of the newts out of the net in his hand. He turned them over and looked at them closely before putting them into the jar.

"Aren't you afraid they will bite you, Uncle George?" Tom asked.

"No, they cannot bite, and for a very good reason. They have got no teeth. They are most harmless creatures.

"But we must be getting home, boys. We have done well for our first visit to the pond. I will tell you all about what we have found when we get home, and you must watch them closely for yourselves."

"Are we going to keep all these animals?" Frank asked.

"We will keep them for a little while, so as to find out what we can about them, then we will put them in the pond again."

CHAPTER VIII

UNCLE GEORGE'S TANK

Uncle George's tank was very simple. It was made up of several large glass bells, such as the gardener uses for covering tender plants.

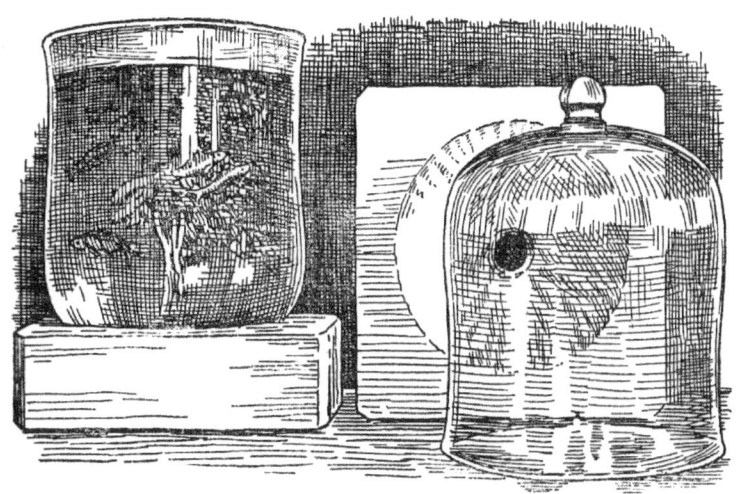

Uncle George's Aquarium

Each glass bell had a nob on the end of it. Uncle George got a large block of wood for each bell-jar. This block he hollowed out with a chisel.

He next bored a large hole in the centre of the

hollow to hold the nob. Then he cut a piece of thick green cloth into a round shape, with a hole in its centre.

This piece of cloth was placed over the hollowed out part of the block, and the bell-jar, turned upside down, was placed in the block so that the glass nob fitted into the hole.

Uncle George fitted up four of these tanks and filled them with fresh water. The frog spawn was put into the first vessel. The next was for the newts. The third one held the caddis worms and some other curious creatures that had been found in the ditch.

In the fourth vessel were half a dozen pretty little fishes called stickle-backs, which the boys had caught in the brook.

Some water weeds and a few water snails or whelks were put into each vessel, except that with the frog spawn in it.

Every other morning Uncle George changed the water by means of a tube which he called a siphon.

Stickle-backs, Pond Weed, etc., in Aquarium

This was a piece of lead pipe, about two

UNCLE GEORGE'S TANK

feet long, and bent in the middle into the form of the letter U.

"The water weeds are very pretty," said Frank.

"They are," replied his uncle, "and they are also very useful. They help to keep the water pure. I should have to change the water every day if there were no weeds in it.

"The whelks also are most useful. They are the roadmen of our ponds and streams. They eat up all the waste matter, and so keep the water clean and healthy."

It was great fun feeding those little fishes. They were fed sometimes on raw meat chopped very fine, sometimes on little pieces of biscuit. At first they were very shy, but they soon got over that. In less than a week they were quite at home, and would come up to the top of the water and take tiny pieces of beef from the boys' fingers.

They would swim after Frank's finger as he drew it round the tank, and would even leap out of the water for food that was held out to them.

At times they darted about as if playing "hide and seek" among the water weeds.

By and by the boys noticed that every time one of the little fish darted at another, the three cruel spines rose up on his back, and that he was really trying to spear his neighbour.

One morning a dead stickle-back was found in the bottom of the tank. A few days later another little fish was picked out pale and stiff.

"They are killing one another," said Frank. "What shall we do?"

"If any more of this fighting goes on we shall have to put them back into the brook," said Uncle George.

"Do they always fight?"

"No, not always—only in spring-time when they are mating. Look! there is one of them getting very pretty. He is the victor—the bully of the pool."

"Let us call him *Bully*," said Dolly; "he is bigger than the others, and oh, so much more beautiful."

Next day another stickle-back was found dead, and Bully's colours were much brighter. He darted about as if the whole tank belonged to him.

He was really a lovely fish now, and he seemed to know it by the proud way in which he dashed about, showing off his fine slender body all shiny with crimson, blue, and gold. He was, as Dolly said, "Just like a little bit of rainbow."

But before the evening a very curious thing took place. Bully seemed to have suddenly lost all his fine colours; and instead of swimming proudly at the top of the tank, he slunk sulky to the bottom.

The strange thing was that *another* stickle-back—a smaller fish than Bully—was now brightly coloured, and seemed to be lord of the tank.

"Bully has been beaten," said Uncle George, "and his victor has taken not only the courage but the colour out of him."

"It serves him right, I think, for being so proud and so cruel. But what is the meaning of all this fighting and change of colours, Uncle George?"

"Oh, it is very simple, Frank. There is a lady stickle-back in the question; and, like the brave knights of old, our little stickle-backs are trying to win her by fighting.

"The victor will marry her. They will build a neat little nest for themselves, and live happily together.

"To-morrow we will take them back to the brook, where the weak ones will be better able to escape.

"In June we will visit the brook. If we are lucky enough to find one of their nests, you will see that after Lady Stickle-back lays her tiny eggs in it, her little husband guards the home night and day.

Stickle-backs and Nest

"When the family are hatching out, the plucky little stickle-back bravely defends the nest.

"He drives away water-beetles, perch, and other fishes much larger than himself. For well he knows that these visitors would quickly gobble up his darlings if they got the chance."

CHAPTER IX

TADPOLES

The frog spawn, when first put into the big glass bell, was just a mass of jelly-like stuff studded all over with black dots.

When looked at closely, it was seen to consist of many round, clear eggs. Each egg was surrounded by a thin skin, and had, in its centre, a little round black ball or yolk.

At the end of a week all these black yolks had lost their round shape. They were now long and oval. During the next four days these oval yolks became little moving animals, each having a head, body, and tail, but no limbs.

From the head of each there grew out two pairs of feathery objects. These, Uncle George told the boys, were gills or breathing organs. Soon another pair of these feathery gills appeared: so that each little creature had now three on each side of his head.

By the end of the second week the little creatures had all wriggled out of the eggs. They hung together by their feathery gills in little black groups.

TADPOLES

"What shall we feed them on?" Frank asked his uncle.

"They are not at all nice in their tastes," Uncle George replied. "They will eat almost anything, from water weeds up to drowned kittens. If they get nothing else, they will eat one another, and not mind it a bit."

"How dreadful," said Frank. "Hadn't we better give them something to eat now, for fear they may eat each other up."

"It wouldn't do much good giving them anything to eat now, for they have *no mouths*."

"No mouths, Uncle George?"

"No mouths," Uncle George repeated. "Is it not curious? For four days the tadpole, or young frog, has no mouth, and yet during that time he grows a great deal.

"Four days after he leaves the egg his mouth appears. It is a very small mouth, fringed with frilled, fleshy lips. These lips are moved by a pair of strong, horny jaws. This mouth is very different from the wide, gaping mouth of the frog."

Just as Uncle George had said, the tadpoles ate nothing for four days. Then their mouths appeared, and they began to eat the water weeds. But Uncle George fed them on raw meat. He said it made them grow quickly. A small piece of raw beef, tied to the end of a string, was lowered into the tank, and the tadpoles swarmed around it. What was left of the beef was pulled out every morning, and a fresh piece put in.

By this means the water was kept clean, and had only to be changed once a week.

"Why, they have no gills now," said Frank one day, as he was helping his uncle to change the water.

"Oh yes, they have, Frank. They have gills like a fish now.

"When they are about four weeks old, their feathery gills go away; but, before this, four gill-slits are formed in each side of the tadpole's head."

Uncle George took a glass tube about twelve inches long, and placing his thumb tightly on one end of it, he pushed it down into the water until the other end was right above a tadpole.

Then he took his thumb off, and the tadpole and some water shot up the tube. He then replaced his thumb tightly on the end of the tube, and lifted it out of the water.

The tadpole and water remained in the tube as long as he kept his thumb on the end of it. He emptied the contents of the tube into a little dish, and Frank looked at the tadpole with a glass.

"I can't see the gill-slits," said Frank.

"Oh yes, you can, if you look closely. What seems to be a big head is really head and body covered over by a cloak of skin."

"Yes, I see the gills now," said Frank. "They are red in colour. I also see the cloak. There is an opening on the left side of it."

TADPOLES

"That is so," said his uncle. "That opening is there to let the water into the gills."

At the end of the fifth week, Uncle George took some tadpoles out for the boys to look at.

"Do you see any change?" he asked.

"Yes," said Tom, "they have two things like hind legs growing out."

"These *are* legs," his uncle said, "and in two weeks from now these legs will have movable joints in them."

Day by day the tadpoles were carefully watched, and the following wonderful changes were observed.

When about seven weeks old, their hind legs became jointed, and long toes were formed. The tadpoles were now able to kick out and swim by means of their long hind legs. Their gills went away, and they came to the surface and took mouthfuls of air. They now had lungs instead of gills.

But the most striking change came at the end of the eleventh week.

One by one they lost the cloak which covered head and body.

Under this cloak a pair of fore legs had been folded up and hidden for some time. They were now tiny, wide-mouthed frogs, with long, clumsy tails.

The clumsy tails grew smaller and smaller daily. At last there was no tail left, and what was at one time a cluster of black, wriggling tadpoles, was now a crowd of lively little dark yellow frogs.

The boys wished to keep them longer, but their uncle told them that they could not do this.

"Your tadpoles are now frogs," he said. "The frog is an insect eater. As we cannot give these little frogs their natural food, we must place them where they can get it for themselves, or they will die."

So the frogs were carried back to their native pond.

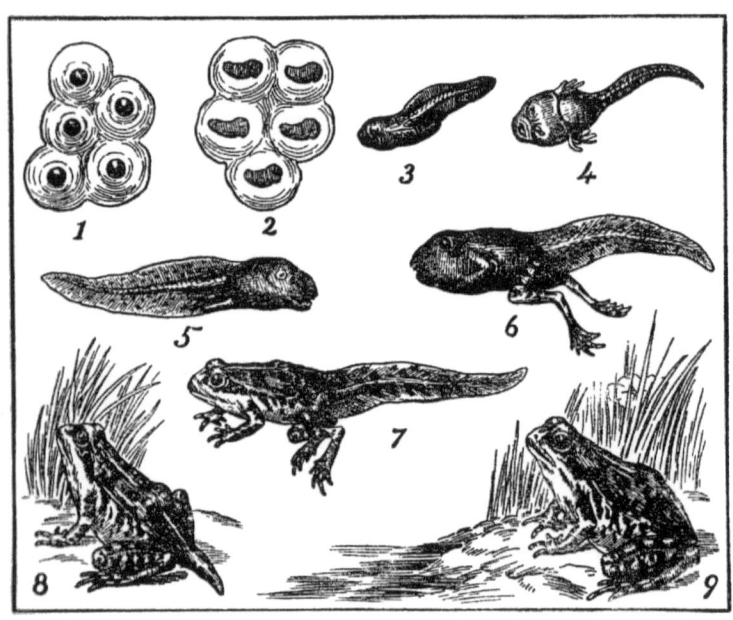

The Development of the Tadpole

1. Portion of Frog Spawn. 2. Same after ten days. 3. A Newly-Hatched Tadpole. The remaining figures show the same Tadpole at (4) one week; (5) three weeks; (6) seven weeks; (7) eleven weeks; (8) thirteen weeks; and (9) fourteen weeks after hatching.

CHAPTER X

FROGS, TOADS, AND NEWTS

"I think we had better take our newts back to the pond now, Frank."

"Oh, do let us keep them for a day or two longer, Uncle George. They are getting quite tame."

As he spoke, Frank drew his finger slowly round the outside of the glass vessel that held the newts. One of the creatures swam round, following his finger.

"Look, Uncle George! He knows me."

"He is hungry, and thinks you ought to have a small worm in your fingers."

"*Thinks*? Uncle George. Can newts *think*?"

"It looks as if they could, does it not? We feed these creatures every day, and they have got into the habit of looking for food every time we come near them. But here comes Tom with the worms."

It was curious to watch how the newt acted when a tiny worm was given it. At first it seemed not to see the worm, although it was wriggling at his nose. It crept back slowly about two or three inches, then all at once it sprang upon the worm and gobbled it up.

"You must tell us all about the newt, Uncle George," said Tom.

"I should like to know how much you two boys have found out by feeding and watching these two," said Uncle George. "So just tell me what *you* know about the newt first, then perhaps I can tell you some things about newts, frogs, and toads which you do not know."

"Well," began Tom, "the newt lives in water. He has four feet, with pretty little toes upon them, and a long tail. He feeds upon worms, tadpoles, and other small animals, and he swallows them whole, because he has no teeth.

"The male has a huge crest, and is gay with bright colours.

Crested Newt, Male and Female

"The female has no crest. She lays her eggs upon the pond weeds. A single egg is laid upon a leaf. The leaf is then rolled round it, so as to hide it from enemies."

"Very good, Tom," said his uncle; "but you have not told us about the newt's skin."

"Oh, I forgot that," Tom went on. "The newt has a

lovely silky skin, which it only wears for about a week, then it casts it off. Now, tell us something more about them, Uncle George."

"The newt does not live in the water all the year," said Uncle George. "During autumn and winter great families of newts sleep together under stones and in dry holes in the earth. They only go to the pond in early spring to lay their eggs."

"Do newts ever become frogs or toads?" asked Frank.

"Oh no, Frank, never. I know what makes you think that. It is because the young frog, just before he loses his tail, is very like a little newt.

"Young newts are tadpoles too, but they differ very much from frog tadpoles. Newt tadpoles live in the pond for more than a year. They have feathery outside gills on all that time. Their *fore* feet are formed first. If you remember, our frog tadpoles got their hind legs first.

"Long ago people believed all sorts of absurd things about the poor, harmless newt. They were afraid to touch it. Every newt found was killed at once, for it was thought to have a sting and poison bag. Even at the present day many people believe that newts and toads are dangerous animals."

"How can you tell a toad from a frog, Uncle George," Tom asked.

"They are very different from each other, both in shape and in their ways of living. The toad is a fat, clumsy animal. His skin is dull and warty. He does not hop, but crawls or walks lazily along.

Frog, Toad, and Newt—showing Eggs of Toad and Newt, and Tadpoles of Frog and Toad

"He lives upon flying insects, which he catches with his curious long tongue. He gets very fat during summer and autumn.

"Before winter comes on, he looks out a snug hole under a root or stone. Here he sleeps the whole winter through.

"In spring he wakes up, lean and hungry, and betakes himself to the pond.

"The eggs of the toad are laid in the water in long strings, each like a double row of beads. They hang gracefully upon the water weeds, and look very pretty.

"The toad tadpoles are very like those of the frog. They go through the same changes.

"The toad also casts his skin, but he does not throw it away like the newt. He takes his old, cast-off skin, rolls it up into a neat little ball, and *swallows it*.

"The frog's body is more slender. His skin is slippery. It is not dull and dingy like that of the toad. It is of a bright greenish yellow colour, marked with black spots of different sizes.

"The frog can change his colour from light to dark. He has long hind legs which enable him to hop very high on land and to swim very fast in the pool.

"He likes the long, damp grass, where he catches flies, beetles, and slugs.

"He sleeps through the winter, buried in the mud at the bottom of the still pool.

"Like the toad, the frog catches his prey by means of a long, sticky tongue, which darts out of his mouth whenever an unlucky insect comes within reach.

"His tongue is fixed to the floor of his mouth just at his lower lip. It is forked at the end. When not in use, it lies folded back inside his mouth and points down his throat."

1. Frog. 2. Toad. 3. Frog catching a Fly with its tongue.

CHAPTER XI

UNDERGROUND STEMS

Uncle George and his three young pupils had been to the woods. After tea he opened the metal box which he carried, slung by a strap over his shoulder, whenever he went out rambling.

This box had in it a pond-net and a couple of wide bottles. To-night it was half filled with plants.

Before laying them on the table, Uncle George washed the soil from their roots at the tap.

"Now then," he said, "let me see how much you remember of our lesson in the woods. I will begin with Dolly"—and Uncle George held up a lovely white flower.

"That," said little Dolly, "is the *wooden enemy*!"

Uncle George laughed loudly, and so did the two

Anemone

boys. Dolly laughed too—she did not quite know why. She was a merry little girl, who laughed whenever she got the chance.

"You mean *wood anemone*, dear, don't you?" said Uncle George, as he stroked her pretty curly hair.

"Yes, I *mean* that, Uncle George; but I can't say it properly," said Dolly, still laughing.

"Oh yes, you can if you try—wood a-nem´-o-ne. It is easily pronounced. Now Frank, it is your turn. What is this one with the great number of yellow petals, the spotted heart-shaped leaves, and the funny fat roots?"

"The pilewort, or lesser celandine," answered Frank.

Marsh Marigold

UNDERGROUND STEMS

"Quite right! Now, Tom, here is one for you. This plant, you see, has broad kidney-shaped leaves with crimped edges, large yellow flowers, and a coarse round hollow stem. We found it, if you remember, growing in the mud at the edge of the brook."

"It is the marsh marigold," said Tom.

"Very good! Now this one?"

As he held it up all three answered at once—"The primrose!"

"We found this one also growing at the edge of the brook." As he spoke, Uncle George held out a very pretty plant. Its flowers were of a pale pinkish blue colour. They were shaped like the flowers of the wallflower, but

Primrose

were smaller. The flowers were borne up upon a long stalk which sprang from a rosette of pretty little leaves.

"It is the *lady's smock*," said Dolly; "I remembered that one because it is so pretty."

"Well done, Dolly!" said her uncle proudly. "Now, I think we have quite enough to go on with. Let us take these up one by one and examine and draw parts of them. First take the wood anemone. What do you call this?"

Uncle George pointed to the stout part of the plant that had been in the ground.

"The root," said Frank.

"No, Frank!" his uncle replied. "But that is what I thought you would say. Now, tell us why you think it is the root."

"Because it grows under ground."

"But roots do not have buds upon them, Frank: and see! flower-stalk and leaf-stalk spring from it, while fibrous, or string like, roots hang down from it."

"It must be a stem, then," Frank ventured.

"It *is* the stem," said his uncle. "We have already seen that the creeping crowfoot and ground ivy have stems that creep along on the surface of the ground.

"Many plants have stems which creep along under ground. This is an underground stem; and this is another." Here he pointed to the primrose.

"Why, I always thought that that pink thing was the root of the primrose," said Frank; "but I see now that it is really more like a stem. It has marks upon it like scars."

"These are marks where leaves once grew upon it," his uncle remarked. "Notice that the primrose leaves form a rosette on the top of this underground stem."

"Is there any reason for these plants having their stems under ground?" Tom asked.

"There is a reason for everything in nature, my boy. Can't you see any reason for this yourself?"

Plants with Underground Stems

"I see one, I think," said Frank; "it enables the plant to creep out to new soil."

"That is one very good reason, Frank. Now, why should it seek other soil?"

"For food!"

"That is right, Frank. Those plants which have underground stems seem to die down every autumn; but they are alive all the time under ground, safe from the frosts and bitter winds which kill tender plants. And they peep up in a new place in spring.

"Now I want you to tell me why these underground stems are swollen out so. It cannot be for strength, for creeping stems don't require to be strong.

"Fetch me a raw potato, Tom, please!

"Now," Uncle George continued, "tell me what this potato is."

"It is an underground stem," said Frank.

"Yes! Why is it swollen? What do we use the potato for?"

"For food. Oh, I know," said Frank, "it is a food store."

"Of course," said his uncle. "It is a supply of food gathered up this year for next year's plant. Look at the roots of the lesser celandine. I see Tom has drawn them. They are swollen. Are they roots, or underground stems?"

"They have neither leaf marks on them, nor buds," said Frank, "I think they must be roots."

"They *are* roots," said Uncle George, "but they are food supplies all the same.

"There are other underground stems that grow quickly. Good examples of these are mint, couch grass, and sand sedge. The underground stems of these plants grow so fast that they are always occupying new ground. They have therefore no need to store up a food supply like their slower growing neighbours the primrose, potato, anemone, iris, and many others."

Pilewort or Lesser Celandine, showing Roots

CHAPTER XII

CATERPILLARS

"We found these upon the dead-nettle." As he spoke, Frank opened a small cardboard box and showed his uncle half a dozen large, hairy caterpillars.

"Splendid," said Uncle George. "We will just put these into the cage."

Uncle George, who was a very good carpenter, had of late been busy in his spare time making a box or cage for keeping caterpillars in. He called it a *larva cage*.

Larva Cage

It was a curious looking thing, something like a small meat-safe. Three sides and the top of it were

CATERPILLARS

covered with gauze. The fourth side was a large pane of glass. The gauze-covered side opposite to this opened as a door.

It was divided into an upper and a lower part by a shelf in the middle, and, by sliding in two pieces of wood, it could be divided into four tiny rooms.

Now that it was finished, Uncle George wanted to get it stocked, and his two nephews wanted it stocked too.

"Do you want any more of these woolly caterpillars?" Frank asked.

"No, Frank, but you can bring me in some more of a different kind. Or, better still, let us go out into the garden now and see if we can find any there."

The gardener beamed with joy when Uncle George told him what they had come to the garden for.

"Caterpillars?" he said. "I wish you would take them all, sir. They are the worst vermin in the garden. Last year they left scarcely a leaf on my currant bushes."

Our three friends went straight to the currant bushes. Here they found a good many pretty little caterpillars of a creamy colour, richly striped with orange, and dotted over with black spots. These, their uncle informed them, were the caterpillars or *larvæ* of the magpie moth.

On the cabbages they found several caterpillars of the large white butterfly. These were bluish green in colour, with three bold yellow stripes running along the whole length of their bodies.

"What are these, Uncle George?" Tom asked, as he turned up a cabbage leaf and pointed to several white patches on its under side. The leaf next it was spotted just like it.

"Oh, Tom, how lucky we are! These are the eggs of the large white butterfly. Now we shall be able to follow up the whole life of this insect, and a wonderful life it is. Let us go right in and examine them. Take some cabbage leaves and some currant leaves to feed the hungry caterpillars with."

"Our larva cage is now quite full," said Uncle George, when he had put the caterpillars in.

"Why do you not put them into the same room, Uncle George?"

"There are two reasons for that, Frank. First, they live upon different kinds of food. The hairy caterpillar, or 'woolly bear,' as boys call it, feeds upon nettles, the cabbage caterpillar prefers cabbage leaves, while the currant caterpillar will only eat currant leaves.

"Second, the woolly bear will sometimes eat up his smooth-skinned friends. Now, get your glasses and have a peep at the beautiful eggs of the 'large white' or 'cabbage' butterfly."

"Why, they are not at all like eggs," said Frank, as he closely looked at them with his glass.

"What are they like, Frank?"

"They are like little pieces of carved ivory all shaped alike," Frank replied.

"Yes, but that does not give us a very clear idea of their shape," observed his uncle. "Come on, Tom."

"They are like little Indian clubs with the handles cut off, only they are beautifully marked with long, slender ridges and cross bars."

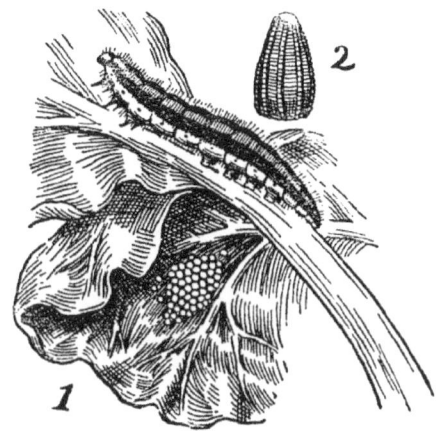

1. *Caterpillar and Eggs of Cabbage Butterfly*
2. *Egg magnified*

"That is really a very good account of them, Tom. They are arranged in patches. Count and let me know how many eggs are in each bunch."

The boys counted all the groups of eggs, and found that there were eight eggs in some, nine in others, but that most of them contained ten or more.

"Now, how many egg patches are there?" asked Uncle George.

"There are seven patches on my leaf," said Frank.

"And ten on mine," added Tom.

"That is about one hundred and fifty eggs altogether," said Uncle George.

"Has each of these bunches of eggs been laid by one butterfly?" asked Frank.

"It is more than probable that one butterfly laid the whole lot," his uncle replied; "for the white butterfly lays, as a rule, over two hundred eggs."

"That is about as many eggs as a hen lays in a year," said Frank.

"Yes," said Uncle George, "a good hen and a white butterfly lay about the same number of eggs in a year; but the butterfly lays all her eggs in one day.

"After laying her eggs, she dies. That is perhaps why she always lays them on the kind of plant which the young caterpillars can feed upon when they hatch out.

"Let us look at the caterpillars now. We need not take them out, as we can easily see them through the glass side of the cage.

"Notice that the body of the cabbage caterpillar consists of a round, dark coloured head and a number of broad, ring-like divisions. How many of these divisions are there?"

"Twelve," said Frank, after counting carefully.

"Right!" said his uncle. "Now, about legs—how many are there?"

"There are three pairs of legs on the first three divisions of its body, and a pair of shorter and stouter legs on each of the sixth, seventh, eighth, and ninth divisions, making seven pairs of legs altogether," Frank answered.

"That is quite correct, Frank, and I am glad you noticed the difference between the first three pairs and the others. The first three pairs are the creature's real legs. The others are false or temporary legs."

"There is a row of black spots on the yellow band along its side," observed Tom.

"These are its breathing-holes, Tom. We breathe by our lungs only, but caterpillars and insects have breathing-tubes all over their bodies."

Caterpillars of Magpie Moth

"The woolly bear and the cabbage caterpillar move about in the same way," said Frank. "But look at those currant caterpillars, Uncle George, what a funny way they have of getting along!"

"These belong to a kind of caterpillars known as 'loopers,'" said his uncle. "They move about by looping up their bodies in this strange manner."

"I do not like to handle those hairy caterpillars," Tom remarked. "Why are they covered with those nasty long hairs?"

"You have just given the reason, Tom. You don't like to touch them on account of these hairs; neither do animals. No bird will eat one of these. If he does, he will never eat another.

"Notice how they coil up like a hedgehog when they

1. Caterpillar, Pupa, and perfect Insect of Tiger Moth
2. Caterpillar, Pupa, and perfect Insect of Magpie Moth
3. White (Cabbage) Butterfly, Male and Female, with Caterpillar and Pupa

are touched. This makes them more difficult to swallow. Just imagine how a bird would feel with one of these ticklish customers stuck in his throat, eh?

"Now, boys, make a sketch of one of the tiny eggs, also one of the big cabbage caterpillar, and then we will go out and have a game of cricket on the lawn."

CHAPTER XIII

THE WHITE BUTTERFLY

Uncle George had to go from home for a week, and his two nephews went part of the way to the railway station with him.

As they were about to take a short cut through the wood, Uncle George went up to a huge beech tree. He looked very closely at its grey trunk for a time, then stepping back from it about three yards, exclaimed:—

"Come here boys! Stand beside me, look closely at this tree, and tell me if you see any strange objects sticking to the bark."

After staring at it for some time, they both declared that they could see nothing upon it.

"Go nearer—nearer still! Now, do you see anything?"

The boys shook their heads.

"Go quite close up to the trunk and examine it," said Uncle George.

"Oh," said Frank suddenly, "I see queer things like grubs, coloured almost exactly like the bark. Some of them are lighter in colour."

"Look carefully at those lighter ones, and you will find that they are just empty cases."

"So they are," said Frank, as he touched one with his finger and saw it crush up.

"Notice how they are fixed to the bark!" said Uncle George.

The boys watched as their uncle placed his pencil under one of the darker coloured objects, and saw that it was slung up to the tree by a loose silken girdle round its middle, while a tuft of fine threads fastened the lower end to the bark.

Suddenly, as if it were annoyed at being touched by the pencil, the lower half of the object moved from side to side with rapid jerks.

"Why, it is alive," said Tom.

"Yes, of course it is," said his uncle. "This is another lucky find."

"What are they?" Frank asked.

"Can't you guess, Frank? Don't you remember my telling you that all the insects were asleep in their cases during winter.

"Each of these darker coloured cases contains a white butterfly. They have been here all winter, and they are just about to hatch out."

"How do you know that, Uncle George?"

"I know it because the empty cases tell me that some of the butterflies have just hatched out. This is what your cabbage caterpillar becomes after he is tired of feeding.

"You have now seen three different stages of the life of this insect. First, the curious eggs laid on the under side of the cabbage leaf; next the greedy caterpillar; and now, the chrysalis or *pupa* stage.

"The caterpillar goes to sleep in autumn as a hard-cased chrysalis, and wakes up in spring a beautiful butterfly."

"How strange," said Frank. "And will our caterpillars remain caterpillars until autumn, and then tuck themselves up like this and go to sleep for the winter."

"No, Frank! our caterpillars will go into the chrysalis state in a week or so, and hatch out as butterflies in August. These August butterflies will lay eggs. The caterpillars from these eggs will turn into *pupæ* in September.

"These September pupæ will supply the white butterflies of next spring and summer. Put some of these into your box. Watch then carefully, and you may be lucky enough to see the white butterfly coming out of his winter case."

"I cannot understand," said Tom, "how a big white butterfly can be inside so small a case. It must be very tightly wrapped up."

"So it is, as you will see," said Uncle George. "Good-bye, boys! and mind, when I come back, I shall expect to see notes and sketches of all that has taken place in the larva cage during my absence."

THE WHITE BUTTERFLY

* * * * * * * * * * * *

"Won't you let your uncle take his dinner first," said Frank's mother, as she hung Uncle George's overcoat up in the hall.

"No, mother! he must come at once," said the excited Frank. "There's a butterfly just coming out."

"Oh, I must come and see that," said Uncle George; and he allowed his eager nephews to drag him towards the larva cage.

By the time they got to the cage the butterfly had hatched, but they were in time to see it unfurl its wings. The wings were crumpled and twisted, but the creature slowly straightened them out to dry in the sun.

"We saw it burst its case," said Tom. "First a small slit appeared at the head end. This slit grew larger. Then the butterfly's head and feet appeared. It squeezed its way and was just half way out, with its wings crumpled round it, when you arrived."

"I arrived just a minute too late, then," said his uncle.

"Oh, and the eggs have hatched too," said Tom. "Look at them now, Uncle George!"

His uncle looked, and saw that the white patches of eggs had given place to larger patches of little active, dark coloured maggots.

"We want to know what has become of the lovely carved shells of the eggs," said Tom.

"They have been eaten up," his uncle replied. "From the moment a caterpillar is born he does nothing but eat—eat—eat. He begins by eating the shell of the egg he comes out of.

"For the first week of their lives these tiny caterpillars feed together in small bands, and they grow so fast you can almost fancy you see them growing. After they have grown to a certain size, each caterpillar starts out for himself."

White or Cabbage Butterfly and Pupa

"Do you see the three butterflies that have hatched out?" asked Tom.

"Yes, I see them. There are two females and one male," said Uncle George.

"How can you tell males from females?" asked Frank.

"Oh, that is easy enough," Uncle George replied.

"The females are larger, and have two big black spots on each of their front wings. But I only see eight of the large cabbage caterpillars. We put in twelve, I think."

"Look!" said Frank, pointing to the roof of the cage.

"Ah, yes, I see them. Two of them have passed into the pupæ stage, and are slung up by their silken belts to the wall of the cage.

"The other two are spinning silken belts round the middle of their bodies, if they have not already done so. After this belt is finished they will slowly slip their useless green skins off, and finally get rid of them by sharply jerking the tail end of their pupa cases."

"Yes, we watched those other two do that," said Tom.

"Notice," continued Uncle George, "that all your big cabbage caterpillars have lost their yellow stripes and are now of a bluish green colour. They have stopped feeding, and are now dull and sleepy. This indicates that they are about to enter the pupa stage."

"But look at the currant and the hairy caterpillars, uncle," said Frank.

"My dear boy," said Frank's mother, "Uncle George must really have food and rest after his long journey. He will hear about the other caterpillars some other time."

CHAPTER XIV

THE TOILING CADDIS

"Look here, boys," said Uncle George, "you have been paying nearly all your attention to the larva cage during my absence, and have forgotten the caddis worms."

Uncle George made believe to be cross.

"We changed the water every two days," said Frank.

"Yes, I know. But you have not reported any changes in the creatures themselves. What has been going on in the larva cage has also been going on here in the water, for caddis worms are simply water-caterpillars. You nearly missed something of very great interest."

Uncle George laid three saucers on the table, and continued:—

"We are going to look into the life of the caddis fly to-day; but before I take them out of the water, I want you to tell me what you have noted about them up to now."

"They are always climbing up the water weeds," said Frank.

THE TOILING CADDIS

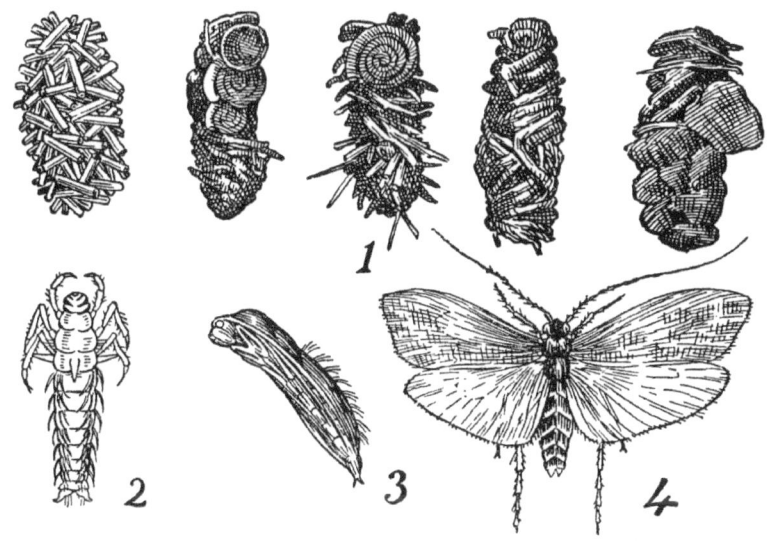

1. Caddis Cases
2. Larva out of Case
3. Pupa
4. Caddis Fly

"They are always adding to their cases," said Tom.

"Some of them have died," said Frank.

"What?" said his uncle. "Do you mean these at the bottom of the tank? These are not dead, they are only asleep. Put your hand in, and take some of these out."

"Their cases are stuck to the pond weeds and to each other," said Frank, as he lifted a few out, and placed them in a saucer.

"Ah, I have it, Uncle George! They have gone into the pupa state. Is that not so?"

Uncle George nodded.

"Look!" exclaimed Tom. "There are things like earwigs floating on the water."

"Never mind these just now, Tom," said his uncle. "I am coming to them by and by. Observe the wonderful cases which the caddis worms have made for themselves.

"Here is one whose case, when we found him, was made of neatly cut pieces of water rush. He has almost doubled the length of his case since then; for see, the front half is made of cut stalks of water weed neatly arranged."

"He has got a fine collar of green pieces round his neck," Frank observed.

"Why are they always adding to the length of their cases?" asked Tom.

"Because they are always growing," said Frank.

"That is the reason," said Uncle George; "and they grow so fast that they have actually to work hard at building.

"Observe those that make their cases out of tiny shells and stones. They have made free use of the coloured beads and small pieces of coal which we put in."

"How do they manage to stick these things together?" asked Tom.

"A caddis worm is a busy creature," his uncle replied. "He does two things besides eating and growing. With those strong pincers, which you see at his head, he saws off pieces of weed.

THE TOILING CADDIS

"Near his mouth he has got a kind of loom for spinning silk. These pieces are stuck together with silk, which is a gluey substance when it first comes from the creature's body.

"These rough cases are lined with silk."

"Why does he have to make a house for himself, and carry it about with him?" said Frank.

In answer to this, his uncle took out a few of the active caddis worms, and placed them in a saucer with water. He held one up.

"You see," he said, "his case is open at both ends. Now, if I tried to get him out from the front, I should never manage it. This is the way to get him out."

As he spoke, Uncle George pushed the head of a pin into the tail end of the case, and the creature scrambled out at once.

"It is too bad turning you out of your cosy room, Mr. Caddis," Uncle George observed; "but you'll go back again as soon as you get the chance, won't you? I want my nephews to understand why you work so very hard.

"Now, Frank, you can answer your own question, I think—'Why does the caddis worm build a house?'"

"Because he has a soft body."

"Quite right. But why is he forced to protect his body?"

"Fishes would eat him."

"Right again, Frank. If trout could speak, they might

tell you that the sweetest morsel in the stream is the caddis worm. Now, take your lens, please, and tell me something about him."

"His body is divided into rings, and there are the same number of them as we found in the caterpillar."

"Very good, Frank. Now give Tom a chance."

"His head and the first three divisions of his body are hard cased. They are black and yellow in colour."

"He has six legs," said Frank, "and they are attached to the first three divisions of his body."

"What about the last division of his body?" Uncle George asked.

"Oh, how funny!" said Frank. "It is divided into two large things like horns."

"These," said his uncle, "are the hooks by which he fixes himself so firmly in his case."

"And what are all these curious big bristles for?" asked Tom. "They are all over his body."

"These are his breathing organs," Uncle George answered. "The caterpillar, if you remember, had breathing-holes along the sides of his body. By moving his long body, the caddis worm causes a constant current of water to pass through his dwelling.

"Look at the fourth segment of his body. How does it differ from the others?"

"It is the broadest segment," said Frank, "and there is a stout rounded thing in the middle of it."

"Yes," his uncle replied, "and if we can get him turned on his back we shall see two more of these stout outgrowths below, one on each side of the same segment. This is really very clever. By it the animal keeps himself in the middle, so that the current of water must flow all around him.

"Now, look at the case of a sleeping caddis."

"The front of the case is closed," said Frank.

"How is it closed, Frank?"

"Well, there is a network of threads over it," answered Frank.

"Yes; you see a caddis worm cannot do without fresh water, even when he is asleep; so, before going to sleep, he builds a grating over the entrance.

"When he wakes up, he has quite a new shape altogether. And this brings us to those things which Tom said were like 'earwigs.' There are five of them floating on the water, and two of these are dead. If you look, you will find five empty caddis cases in the tank."

"How does he get out of the case?" inquired Tom.

"Easily enough. Look at the strong pair of pincers he has got for cutting his way through the silken grating with. No longer burdened with his heavy case, he floats up to the surface. He crawls up out of the water into the air.

"If there are no rushes or floating leaves about, he is sure to drown; for your caddis is no longer a water insect, but a fly inside a thin skin.

"Now, boys, I am going to show you something wonderful."

Uncle George then took out the three living pupæ that were floating on the water, and placed them on the table. The boys watched them for a long time.

They were beginning to get impatient, when suddenly the skin of one of the creatures burst along the back, and a lovely little fly, with brown, gauzy wings and long feelers, came out.

After airing its wings for about a minute, it flew to the window. The other two acted in just the same way.

"Now, my dear boys, I think you know something about the life of the caddis fly. For a whole year of his life he is a crawling water insect, then, for about a single day, he is a lively fly."

"How does the caddis larva first get into the water?" asked Frank.

"As an egg, Frank. The female caddis fly lays her eggs in the water. She sometimes even crawls down right into the water to lay them.

"A tiny caddis grub, no bigger than this pin-head, comes out of each egg. As soon as he hatches out, he begins to build his case, to eat, and to grow; and from the moment of his birth up to the closing up of his tube, he is scarcely a moment idle."

APPENDIX
HINTS TO TEACHERS

BUDS.—Twigs of beech, horse-chestnut, lilac, and hawthorn ought to be taken in in December and placed in water. They should have as much warmth and light as possible.

Willow twigs (for catkins) might also be forced in this way.

SEEDS.—Seeds should be soaked for twenty-four hours and then sown in sawdust in boxes 4 inches deep. They should be sown in presence of the pupils.

In winter these boxes should be kept on the hot pipes in school. The sawdust should not be allowed to get dry, neither should it be deluged with water, but kept evenly moist if possible.

Be careful to use water *not colder than the temperature of the room* in which the seeds are grown. Nothing checks growth more effectively than chilling with icy-cold water. It is a good plan to keep the watering-pan full of water near the hot pipes, refilling it always after use.

Seeds germinate best in the dark, but whenever the plumule shows above the sawdust, the box containing them should be placed in the light. Sufficient seeds should be sown at one time to supply a plant to each pupil once a week for at least four weeks. A number of seeds or plants should be dug up once a week and sketched by the children. Each sketch should be compared with that of the previous week, and all changes duly noted down.

The best seeds to grow are:—Broad bean, common or "large white" maize, runner bean ("Painted Lady"), French bean, kitchen pea ("Stratagem"), and white mustard.

A few seeds of white mustard should be sprinkled on a small piece of moist blotting-paper, and covered over by a small glass bell-jar or an inverted tumbler. In less than a week the root-hairs may be seen.

If hot-water pipes are available, the following seeds should be grown, as their germination is interesting:— date stones, walnuts, chestnuts, almonds, cherry stones, orange pips, seeds of cucumber and sunflower.

After maize and bean (or pea) plants have reached the height of 5 inches, they should be transferred to bottles of tap water—as described at the end of Lesson VI—and the continuous growth sketched and noted from week to week.

POND AND DITCH HUNTING.—Make a ring of stout brass wire about 8 or 10 inches in diameter, and to this attach a bag net made of mosquito netting not more than 9 inches deep. In making the wire ring, leave attached to it about 5 inches of the twisted ends of the wire. Such a net as this can be easily carried and quickly attached to the end of a walking-stick by means of a piece of string.

APPENDIX

The best "finds" are often made by sweeping the net under banks and among pond weeds.

FROG SPAWN.—Frog spawn is abundant in ponds and ditches everywhere in March. It should be kept immersed in as much water as possible in a large vessel, preferably of glass. Whenever the water show signs of fouling, it should be changed; but, as changing water containing tadpoles is somewhat difficult, the fewer changes the better.

As in the case of seed growing, the development of the tadpole should be learnt by weekly sketches and notes.

NEWTS.—Newts can be taken with the gauze-net or in the following way:—Tie a piece of small worm on to the end of a cotton thread fastened to the end of a willow or hazel switch. Cast into the part of the pond where the newts are, and await results.

Live newts, fish, frog spawn, etc., may be obtained from Messrs Willson, Live Stock Providers, 37 New Oxford Street, London; Thomas Bolton, 25 Balsall Heath Road, Birmingham, and other dealers. Newts should be fed once a day on pieces of small worms.

CATERPILLARS.—Caterpillars and pupæ, if not obtainable in local woods, fields, and gardens, can be had from Messrs Watkins & Doncaster, 36 Strand, London, and others.

CADDIS LARVÆ.—Caddis worms are to be found in almost every stream, pond, and ditch. Most of them are vegetable feeders: therefore a plentiful supply of water weeds should be placed in their tank. Carnivorous caddis worms may be fed on small pieces of raw meat. (See Stickle-backs.)

STICKLE-BACKS.—Stickle-backs are common in canals and streams. They are easily caught with the net. They should be fed once a day on grated biscuit, and occasionally on raw meat. The meat should be chopped very fine, and then pressed through a piece of perforated zinc. Very little food suffices. If too much is put in, the residue should be removed by means of a glass tube, as described in Lesson IX. If no green water plants are obtainable, the water should be changed at least every second day by means of a siphon. Once a month is quite often enough if sufficient green plants are kept in the tank and decaying matter carefully removed. Do not over-stock—few fishes and much water is the rule.

WATER PLANTS.—It is best to take the water plants which are found growing locally. The following are fairly common:—*Elodea canadensis,* water millfoil; *Potamogeton* (*nitens, crispus,* or *filiformis*), "water soldier"; *Vallisneria spiralis, Chara, Nitella,* water star-wort and watercress. A good selection of excellent aquarium plants are advertised at a cheap rate by the Solway Fishery Co., Dumfries. Water plants, if not rooted in the tank, should be renewed occasionally.

LARVÆ CAGE.—Take four square pieces (about 1½ inches square) of wood, each a foot long, and nail or screw them upright into the four corners of a square piece of ¾-inch deal measuring a foot each way. Stretch mosquito netting over sides, end, and top, arranging

APPENDIX

that one side can be opened. This can be managed by fastening the last fold of netting to one of the upright posts by three drawing-pins. Fresh leaves should be supplied daily. For those caterpillars which pupate in the soil, a shallow earthenware flower-pot—known in the trade as a "seed-pan"—should be supplied. The seed-pan should be filled with soil, the pupæ placed on the surface, and a layer of moss placed over them. Once a week the moss should be dipped in water, squeezed almost dry, and replaced on the pupæ.

AQUARIUM.—Procure from a local florist or seedsman what is known as a "propagating bell." These cost from 1s. up to 2s. 6d. A block of wood 12 inches square and 4 or 5 inches in thickness is also required. Bore a hole about 2 inches in diameter right through the centre of the block, to hold the knob of the bell. Then, with a gouge chisel, make a saucer-shaped hollow round the hole, to roughly fit the rounded end of the bell. Before fitting the bell into the block, interpose a thin layer of moss.

This makes an excellent aquarium—elegant and serviceable. Keep the aquarium in a window, but shade it from bright sunlight.

EXERCISES

CHAPTER I

1. Write out the names of all the wild birds you have seen.

2. Some of these we do not see in winter. How is this?

3. Why should we remember the birds in winter-time?

4. Describe the robin. How does he differ from the bullfinch?

CHAPTER II

1. Why do we put out suet and scraps of meat for certain birds in winter?

2. How can you tell a flesh-eating from an insect-eating bird?

3. Write down the names of all the birds which belong to the crow family.

4. What makes the jackdaw steal all his food?

5. Why are jackdaws, rooks, sparrows, starlings, and blackbirds said to be "the farmer's friends"?

APPENDIX

CHAPTER III

1. Take in twigs with buds on them in December. Place them in water, and watch them from day to day.

2. Select one bud, and make a drawing of it every third day from the time it begins to open. Keep your drawings.

3. How are buds protected? (1) from cold; (2) from animals.

4. What causes the "horse-shoe" marks on horse-chestnut twigs?

5. Make a drawing of a small beech twig, showing buds and leaf-scars.

CHAPTER IV

1. Soak some seeds of broad bean (or pea) and maize (or wheat) for twenty-four hours. Plant some in damp sawdust.

2. What do you see when you open a bean seed?

3. Pick off the little baby plant, and try to draw it big.

4. Cut down through the centre (flat side) of a maize seed. Try to make out the little seed plant and the food store.

5. Every third day dig up a growing seed and draw it. Put the date beneath each drawing. Keep your drawings carefully.

CHAPTER V

1. Explain all that happens when a horse-chestnut bud opens.

2. Why do the buds which you force indoors wither after they open?

3. What changes come over your bean seeds as they grow?

4. Do the young plants draw any food from the sawdust? If not, what feeds them?

5. What three things does a seed need in order to start growing?

CHAPTER VI

1. Make sketches of a soaked bean and of a soaked maize seed.

2. Place a few beans (or peas) and a few maize (or wheat) seeds in a box of damp sawdust. Water regularly. After a week dig up a seed of each and draw them.

3. Dig up a seed of each at intervals of two weeks, three weeks, and four weeks; draw and compare them.

4. Sow in a box of sawdust a few of each of the following—date stones, orange pips, walnuts, chestnuts. Keep the box in a *warm* place, and watch how these seeds grow.

APPENDIX

CHAPTER VII

1. What did the boys find in the pond?

2. What other living things may be seen in ponds? Make a list of all the pond creatures you know.

3. Why do caddis "worms" build cases round themselves?

4. Can newts bite? Give reason.

CHAPTER VIII

1. What is an aquarium?

2. Why are water weeds and water snails put into an aquarium?

3. How do you feed small fish? Why should you be careful not to put in more than the fishes can eat?

4. Where does the stickle-back lay its eggs?

CHAPTER IX

1. What are tadpoles?

2. How old is the frog before his hind legs appear?

3. A tadpole seems to be all head and tail. Can you explain this?

4. How do tadpoles breathe—(1) when they are first

hatched? (2) when they are four weeks old? (3) when they are eleven weeks old?

CHAPTER X

1. Where are frogs, newts, and toads in winter-time?

2. How could you tell a toad from a frog?

3. What is the difference between young newts (tadpoles) and young frogs (tadpoles)?

4. Write the life of a frog (or of a toad) as if told by the creature itself.

CHAPTER XI

1. Dig up a primrose plant, and make a rough sketch showing underground stem, roots, and leaves.

2. An underground stem may be of use to a plant in three different ways. Can you name them?

3. There are two distinct kinds of underground stems—those that grow quickly and those that grow slowly. Name three of each kind, and tell how they differ in shape.

4. Compare a potato with a horse-chestnut twig. Supposing your twig to be swollen out with plant-food, what parts of it do the "eyes" of the potato represent? What do the (scars/marks) near the "eyes" represent?

APPENDIX

CHAPTER XII

1. Where would you look for the eggs of the white butterfly? Why are they always laid upon the same kind of plant, and why *under* the leaf?

2. Explain how caterpillars breathe.

3. Take any caterpillars you find. Observe the leaves you find them feeding upon. Give them fresh leaves every day, and watch how they grow.

4. Why has the "woolly bear" caterpillar got a hairy coat? What does he usually feed upon?

CHAPTER XIII

1. Explain why the pupæ of white butterflies are coloured like the objects they are attached to.

2. Write the life of a white butterfly, and illustrate your description with sketches of caterpillar, pupa, and butterfly.

3. The life of an insect is divided into four distinct stages. Name them. Which is the longest stage in the case of the white butterfly?

4. Describe, as you have observed it, the behaviour of a caterpillar as it passes from the larva to the chrysalis form.

CHAPTER XIV

1. Turn a caddis worm out of his case in the way described in the lesson. Place the insect in a saucer half filled with water, and make a rough sketch of it.

2. When you have finished your sketch, place the empty caddis case in the saucer, and watch how the creature gets into it.

3. Make two columns by drawing a line down the centre of a page of your note-book. In the first column, describe the structure of the caddis larva and fly; in the second, that of the cabbage caterpillar and butterfly. Compare them.

4. In the same way describe the *mode of life* of the caddis fly (Column 1), and of the white butterfly (Column 2).

www.ingramcontent.com/pod-product-compliance
Lightning Source LLC
Chambersburg PA
CBHW042309150426
43198CB00001B/15